Predators

Ian Rohr

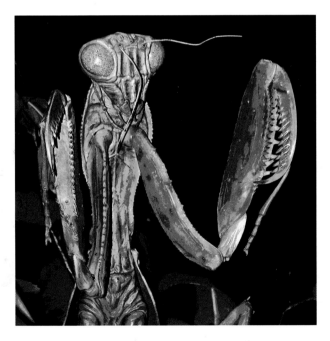

Blake
EDUCATION

Lexile® measure: 550L
For more information visit: www.Lexile.com

Brainwaves Blue
Predators
ISBN 978 1 86509 924 8

Blake Education Pty Ltd
ABN 50 074 266 023
Locked Bag 2022
Glebe NSW 2037
Ph: (02) 8585 4085
Fax: (02) 8585 4058
Email: info@blake.com.au
Website: www.blake.com.au

Series publisher: Katy Pike
Series editors: Sophia Oravecz and Garda Turner
Designer: Cliff Watt

Picture credits: pgs 15 (top), 16, 17 (bottom),
27 photolibrary.com.

Printed by Thumbprints UTD

CONTENTS

Catch, Kill and Eat

Imagine if everywhere you went something tried to eat you.

Predators catch, kill and eat other animals. So watch your back when you go outside. Make sure nothing's hunting you!

Let's journey into the deadly world of predators.

Praying Predators

Lions, tigers, crocodiles and sharks are well-known predators. But predators come in all shapes and sizes. And they're all looking for a feed.

Fast food

Praying mantises take their time. Sitting quite still on a leaf, they watch and wait. A bug passes by. The mantis strikes, catching its prey with sharp spikes on its front legs.

Q: What did the mantis say to the beetle?
A: *Stop bugging me.*

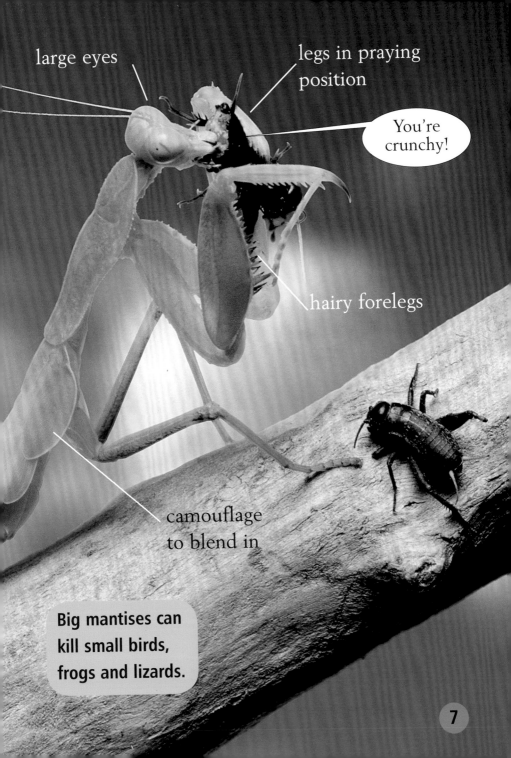

large eyes

legs in praying position

You're crunchy!

hairy forelegs

camouflage to blend in

Big mantises can kill small birds, frogs and lizards.

I'm coming to get you.

Flying Feeders

It is night. Some predators are just waking up. Hundreds of insect-eating bats fly out of dark caves. They are going hunting.

One bat senses movement on a branch. It's the praying mantis eating a bug. The bat swoops, grabbing the mantis in its sharp teeth. After eating the mantis, the bat flies off. It has much more hunting to do.

They want your blood

Vampires do exist! At night, vampire bats come out of their caves. They are looking for blood. Their small, sharp teeth cut into the veins of sleeping animals. Even people!

Vampire bats don't kill their prey. But they can carry the deadly disease called rabies.

Strike Force

Dawn nears. The bat heads home with a belly full of bugs. But it has a visitor. A snake lies in wait outside the bat's cave.

The bat's wings touch the snake. The snake strikes. It injects **venom** into the bat. The strong poison kills quickly. The snake then swallows the bat whole.

Hugged to death

1 Constrictors don't use poison.
2 A constrictor bites its prey. It winds its body around the mouse. Every time the mouse breathes out, the snake squeezes tighter.
3 The mouse can't breathe. It dies and is eaten.

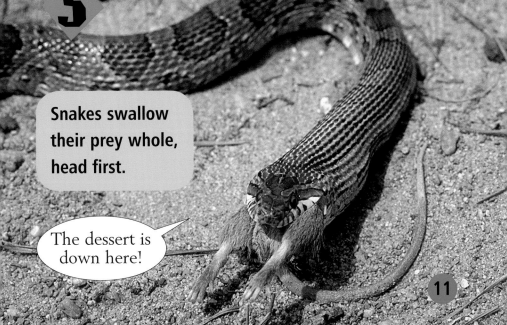

11

12

Look Out—Predators About!

Do you feel safer in a group?

Large herds of grass eaters live on the African plains. Look closely and you'll see predators watching them. If an animal is too busy eating, a bit slow or sleepy, this might be the last day of its life!

A Dangerous Journey

Wildebeest and zebra herds travel long distances looking for food. This annual journey is called a **migration**.

A large herd of wildebeest comes to a wide river. The animals at the front stop. They don't want to enter the river. But they can't turn back. They are pushed on until suddenly a group **plunges** into the water. The river crossing has begun.

A short life

Many young wildebeest don't survive. The small, wobbly calves are easy pickings for predators. Luckily, thousands are born at the same time. The predators can't eat them all!

Hey! Stop pushing!

Jaws of Death

The crocodiles move in.
The crocodile leaps out of the water and grabs the wildebeest by the head. It then pulls the animal down under the water.

Yipes!

The wildebeest kicks and **bellows** to try to free itself. It is no match for the crocodile's strong jaws. The wildebeest drowns and the crocodile has its meal.

Crocodiles usually catch their prey when animals come down to rivers to drink.

Croc and roll

The death roll is deadly. The crocodile pulls the animal under the water. Then, it spins the animal around and around. This drowns the prey quickly. Very few animals escape.

A Pack of Predators

A pack of **hyenas** is on the hunt.
The wildebeest herd panics!

Some of the herd run away from the river. The hyenas follow. The hyenas quickly target a young wildebeest. The calf is scared. It tries to rejoin its mother but the hyenas cut it off. They pile onto the terrified animal and tear it to pieces.

Hyenas are pack animals. This means that they live, and hunt, in groups.

Hide and Eat

The wildebeest herd scrambles up the muddy river bank. Most of them have survived the crocodiles. Now they have to face a new set of predators. Hiding low in the bushes, two lions wait.

The lions charge! Again the predators pick out a young or a weak one. After the kill, other lions rush over to share the meal.

The rest of the wildebeest are safe — for now.

I'm training to run faster!

Lions like to hide near a waterhole. There is always a lot to eat at the waterhole.

predator	prey	when	amount
bats	insects	per night	3 000
tigers	meat	per meal	7 – 27 kg
orcas	seals, sharks, penguins	per day	230 kg

How a lion gets its lunch

A lion has to work hard to eat zebra. Zebras are big animals with bone-breaking hooves. The lion drags the zebra down and bites its throat. The zebra can't breathe and dies.

Tiny Terrors

Could you eat a horse?

If a shrew was as big as you it could eat a horse. Shrews eat their own weight in food every day. This would be the same as you eating 300 hamburgers a day!

All You Can Eat

Shrews are tiny animals, but they have big bellies. These **insectivores** must eat all night just to stay alive. A shrew can starve to death in 12 hours!

Attack of the Killer Shrews

Shrews are known as vicious, little animals. A 1959 horror movie, *Killer Shrews*, had people trapped on an island with 300 giant, hungry shrews!

This means big trouble for any small creature a shrew meets. Most of the time shrews eat insects. But they'll also kill and **devour** snakes, spiders, frogs, mice and even other shrews.

I'm hungry!

Shrews have a long, thin nose called a snout and a mouth full of small, sharp teeth.

A Night to Go Hunting

Shrews love the dark. Like many predators, shrews do most of their hunting at night. They are **nocturnal**.

Two's a crowd

Shrews are solitary animals; they like to live on their own. If two shrews are put together, they will fight to the death. Then, the winner will eat the loser!

I can only lose once!

Shrews have tiny eyes so they can't see well. Instead, they use their big ears to hear their prey. And, their keen sense of smell helps them sniff out food.

Shrews will attack, kill and eat animals 10 times bigger than themselves.

The Hunter Becomes the Hunted

Small predators have to be careful too. When they are out hunting, so are other, bigger creatures. And some of these like shrew for supper.

Hawks use their excellent eyesight to spot prey far below.

Owls, hawks, cats, snakes and **weasels** are all happy to hunt shrews. In the animal world it's eat or be eaten. That's why they call it a food chain.

food chain

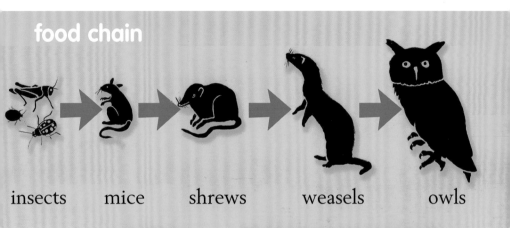

| insects | mice | shrews | weasels | owls |

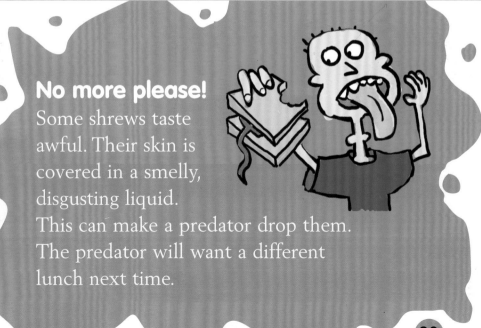

No more please!

Some shrews taste awful. Their skin is covered in a smelly, disgusting liquid.
This can make a predator drop them. The predator will want a different lunch next time.

Fact File

Cookie-cutter sharks leave some food for later. They bite a circle of flesh out of whales and dolphins.

Mmmmm . . . cookies!

Orcas, or killer whales, come right up onto a beach to catch seals. They use the next wave to get back out to sea.

Some spiders, and other insects, eat their prey from the inside out. They suck out the insides, leaving a hollow shell.

It's just like a milkshake.

Glossary

bellows   loud cries of pain or fear

devour   to eat

frantic   wild with fear or pain

hyenas   dog-like predators that live in large packs or groups

insectivores predators that live mainly on insects

migration   a long journey done every year

plunges   throws oneself into something

venom   a poison used by some animals to kill their prey

weasels   small predators that live mainly on rats, mice and rabbits

wildebeest   large African antelopes, also known as gnus

Index